CANBERRA LIGHT

By the same author

Poetry
The Wolf Problem in Australia (1994)
Backpack Despatches: Travel Poems (1998)
The Impatient World (2002)
A Constellation of Abnormalities (2017)

Chapbooks
Vanuatu Moon (vols 1 & 2: 2011 / 2012)
Greenhouse: the Penguins Revolt & Other Poems (Sample selection) (2015)

(As compiling editor:)
Little Book of Childhood (2003)
Birds: Poems by Judith Wright (new supplemented edition, 2003)

Plays
Deadline: A Manual for Hostage-Taking
A Galah in the Samovar

Non-fiction (As compiling editor:)
Acquired Tastes: Celebrating Australia's Culinary Culture (1998)
A Sporting Nation: Celebrating Australia's Sporting Life (1999)
The Endless Playground: Celebrating Australian Childhood (2000)

CANBERRA LIGHT

Poems on the capital and region

PAUL CLIFF

RECENT
WORK
PRESS

Canberra Light: Poems on the capital and region
Recent Work Press
Canberra, Australia

Copyright © Paul Cliff, 2019

ISBN: 9780648553731 (paperback)

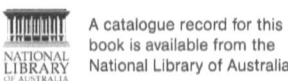
A catalogue record for this book is available from the National Library of Australia

All rights reserved. This book is copyright. Except for private study, research, criticism or reviews as permitted under the Copyright Act, no part of this book may be reproduced, stored in a retrieval system, or transmitted in any form by any means without prior written permission. Enquiries should be addressed to the publisher.

Cover Image © Paul Cliff, 2019
Author photograph by Skye Blomfield (taken at the National Arboretum, Canberra)
Cover design: Recent Work Press
Set by Recent Work Press

recentworkpress.com

The writing of some of these poems was assisted by a writing grant from artsACT in 2011.

Supported by

*For my daughters, Hannah and Ursula.
Raised in this fine town, and sharing in many of these
places and experiences*

Contents

THE CITY

Canberra light	3
Meditation: The idea of law and order	5
Blótmonath	7
Tuggeranong: The hills	8
Squeegee	9
Trompe l'oeil: miracle off Northbourne	10
Ecology	11
Gang-gang	12
Lament: the lake, the reef	13
Captain Cook Memorial Water Jet Variations	14
1. Saturation (the pedal-boat)	14
2. Runaway (*Après toi, le déluge?*)	14
3. Fantasy: the waterspout, the carp, the Parliament	15
Rowing Song	16
Eights training	16
Postscript: the coxswain's story	18
Sacrificials 1 & 2	19
1. The dying place	19
2. All the pretty, drowned horses	20
'Rusty'	21
The *1812* on Anzac Parade	22
Papuan post-figures	23
Vale, National Tally Room	24
Mexican wave	25
Aquarium songs	26
Freshwater species ('Riverland')	26
Murray Cod	26
Marine species	27
Cupcake	28
Getting the drift	29
Ode to *Skywhale*	31
King parrots' descent	32
Two elegies	33
Bringing down the gum	33
The cleansing	34
Bush news	35
Mount Majura prayer: Summer	35
Cockatoo evening	36
Lester Young plays the Top Dam	37

CAPITAL & REGIONAL CONUNDRUMS

Canberra: A defence	41
Gridlock arrives in the Capital	41
The flag ('Summer Holiday'?)	42
Song: Spring-thing	42
Mitchell's Cure (Or 'So long and thanks for all the fish'): A true story	43
Lament: The servos	43
The bunnies	44
Summernats redemption (Or: 'Hey, we do hoon here, too!')	44
Hibernation	44
Painting the elephant	45
Wetsuit: the corrections	45

OVER THE MOUNTAINS TO THE SEA

Two takes on Weereewa	49
Weereewa (aka 'George')	49
Double-take: Chaplin encounters 'King' Yates on Lake George	50
The Snowy also rises. (The pollinators)	51
Instructions for walking mountain country	52
Kosciuszko Report	54
Bushfire season: the comedians	56
Daytrip to the snowfield	57
Easter Sunday Morning, 'Nil Desperandum'	58
In Nimmitabel (Or: the Monaro gets its elephant)	59
Four sketches of Monaro towns	60
1. Diaspora: Adaminaby Blues	60
2. Nimmitabel News (or: Don't frighten the horses)	60
3. Off-season Blues	61
4. Lake Eucumbene Gothic	61
Salmon trout	62
Beach house	64
Crow	65
At Mogo Zoo (The rhino, the meerkats)	66
Gulls' hornpipe	67
Sea salmon's ovation	68
The fleet	69
The crèche	70
Community	71

Afterword	72

THE CITY

Canberra light

Don't tell us about the light. We already know
of the infinite and subtle array of ways it falls on this countryside,
to enchant us time and again. That it's just the everyday leisurewear
of these valleys, hills and plains. The routine, instinctive thing,
this landscape will do when left to its own recourse.
Whether we happen to be watching on, or not.

Yes: Glorious light descends—breaks, bursts, spills,
pours and shatters itself. Abounds all around, in a way which by rights,
should startle us every time. And often will do.
As we casually gaze eastward while crossing Kings Avenue Bridge in our car
to take in the shadows dappling the round hills above Queanbeyan.
Look down upon Civic's distant huddle
while sat hip-to-hip with the dog on the Mount Majura walking trail.
Meditate lakeside, mesmerised by the water's intense reflection,
slip-sliding and toppling as it wrestles and takes tension
with the deep stillness of itself ...
And likewise, all the countless other times—various aspects, occasions
and situations—when we find ourselves startled and ravished
by light anew. However it chooses to come:

>Brandished far out to the south,
>on the wagon-circle of the Brindabella Range.
>Frogmarched up the fire-blackened flank of Mount Stromlo.
>Sung from hilltop to hilltop like giddy roundels.
>Hovering on-high like a wrecked mothership
>to haemorrhage in great silky gold skeins through cloud-shoals ...
>Belly-crawling its way in to us over the big limestone plain
>to king-hit the lake, and ignite the promenade's stunned ranks
>of Manchurian pears in a dazzling fusillade.
>Or infiltrating the city at dusk: goose-stepping the long, broad, straight
>avenues, to enfold Civic's small nest of office blocks in a giddy lasso.
>Holding them safely there—corralled like water, or prayer.
>Cupped in its glistening hands.

Yes, just as you say: This place has spectacular light.
It's as if, were the city not there, people would still have to come and gather
to stare at this landscape anyway. And if, at times, those of us privileged
to live with this spectacle day-to-day
might sometimes appear jaded, inured, blasé, or even immune to light's play—

nonetheless, in the end—when all's broken down and accounted for
(and even for those of us who might not admit it to ourselves)—
it would have to be said that the light here puts heart in us all.
And forms some fair-and-reasonable, vital part of the reason we stay.

Meditation: The idea of law and order

(Dusk, from Mount Majura)

Parliament's outsize flag flies from its bunker
in the Versailles-scale lawns of Capitol Hill:
apex of The Triangle, and hub of the city's orderly wheel—
while arrayed in a great arc all around,
the Public Service's office blocks wind their day down
from transacting the manifold, necessary deals
to oil the cogs of the common weal.
And what passes for this city's peak-hour
is now muscling up in the dusk
to nudge its way home along Northbourne Avenue.
Eased through the lights and roundabouts,
drifting on to the satellite suburbs floating out
in the further valleys and fields.
As the red-&-white lights on Mounts Ainslie and Majura
commence to blink and carousel from high-point to high-point.
As if to warn the citizenry off
flying into its own hills.

Still, despite this intended order and exactitude,
there are always freelance miscreants
to sow some healthy, random discord.
These white cockatoos, for instance—
shambling their slovenly way round the evening skies.
Criss-crossing the neighbourhood in aimless gyres,
with the vaguest taint of menace at their edge:
like an occupation force which might succumb
to sacking and looting. Impulsively setting fire
to houses and lawns, apartment blocks and shopping malls.

And, likewise, their slim-shouldered confederates, the roos:
breaching their reserve to gently crash down
from the light-timbered hills, like this one I'm standing on now.
Infiltrating the zone, to slip through the neat-combed streets
and haul to, upright, like hesitant prayers
or bend deer-like to tug at the couch and fescue
of the nature strips and playing fields.

Yes—train the City as you will out along its axes and avenues,
the rules will always be broached
by the dyed-in-the-bone mavericks,
free spirits and rogue individualists
operating at a sly tangent to this world.
The roos and cockatoos just don't give a damn
for good governance, order; for Griffin or The Plan.
Penalise, tax and legislate—regulate all you will.

Blótmonath

(Autumn from Telstra Tower, Black Mountain. 878 m asl)

November was 'Blótmonath', the Anglo-Saxon's
'Month of Blood Sacrifice': of cattle principally, but occasionally human.
And looking down onto this May landscape now,
there's just the vaguest hint of ritual and bloodletting *here* too.
Sacrifice made to some solar or lunar deities.
Propitiations torn from the pages of Frazer's *Golden Bough*,
for preserving the ongoing cycles of Life and Death.
Acknowledging waning and decay. Regeneration, fruitfulness and renewal.

Aspen Island, stood on its hobbled banks of mournful,
dipping willows, and centred by its menhir-Carillon,
might be venue for sacrificing a hemp-skirted maiden
with flowers woven in her intricately braided hair.
A bog-man might be disinterred from the peaty ground
of the Patrick White Lawns:
fine-creased lines on the smiling half-moons of his eyelids.
Strong, tanned throat snugly slit, ear-to-ear,
and wrists bound behind, in a kind of reverse, pagan-prayer.
Sacrificed up to the Brutal architecture of the place.
A chieftain might be dug from the Reconciliation Place barrow:
complete with the skeleton of his favourite horse,
withered iron sword, and rotted wood shield.
Or a buried ship might secret itself
on the high spot of Springbank Island,
between the Yarralumla Yacht Club and the rowing course.
Awaiting discovery still, like those disclosed
at Walkington Wold, Prittlewell and Sutton Hoo.

Yes, if you lend yourself, such thoughts can obliquely suggest themselves,
here in the willowy, misty landscape of this Cool Temperate zone,
at this time of year. Given a trick of the light, the right whim or mood—
as you look out from the Telstra Tower down onto the great-wheeling
planned city triangulated below. Set round its postmodern paleo-lake.
Entangled in Griffin's Plan, like Glastonbury in its ancient ley lines.
As the city's traffic now commences banking up along Commonwealth Avenue,
to creep its penitent way across the face of the darkening, concreted moorscape
lit up like a peak-hour procession of Druids.

Tuggeranong: The hills
(1998)

For a feel of the city's full measure, we drove south
over the lake one day our first week here:
out across the Limestone Plains, along Drives, Avenues, Parkways ...
Running all the way, to end up in some neonate satellite-suburb
called Tuggeranong.
Huddled like a wagon-circle round a small feature lake,
and looking as raw-boned in all the bald waste, as Fort Dodge in 1868.
Bare-scraped clay paddocks tentatively staked out with surveyors pegs,
the foundations of some prospective IGA and (already operative) bottle shop.
With a billboard touting some future grand vision called 'Hyperdome',
coming soon. Then, persevering a few kilometres more,
we arrived at an historical homestead,
with its white gateposts raised like hands in pale protest,
begging for the City to please stop.

One suburb this way had streets with painters' names
(Nolan, McCubbin, Dobell and the like),
with the streets growing increasingly cribbed
as the planners seemingly ran out of canvas to work.
Housing stock shunted hard up onto a Telstra phone-tower:
looking in the barren, hostile surrounds
like some North-West citadel out of Kipling's *Kim*.
All the bob-catting tradesmen busy bullying the gardens, driveways
and pocket lawns from the reluctant clay
hardly having room to turn their utes around
for home when they knocked off work.
With yet smaller-and-meaner streets to come
(and be allocated more minor painters' names you'd presume):
Pro Hart Passage and Rolf-Harris Laneway coming here soon?

Then, just when the sense of claustrophobia had peaked,
your car came to a halt at a dead-end street—
and you lifted your eyes high over the steering wheel,
to suddenly behold what no planners, developers or builders
could ever reach, tame, stain or desecrate:
the up-swell of the Brindabella Range,
and the snow on the Alps' foothills behind.

Squeegee

(Squeegee and flowers gaffertaped to traffic lights, cnr Barry Drive and Northbourne)

Greyhound thin, with long matted beard and hair
(each successive summer and winter
seeming to discover him more bent and lean),
he could have a menacing way of coming at you
with his sidewards scowl, and brusque, insistent jerk of the head.
As he lurched himself at your windscreen,
whether this was a thing which you actually wanted or not.
Leaning across your car's hood, one raptor elbow winged out
to scrape at an ornery bird-mark with the heel of a fisted hand—
before either nodding and discreetly palming your coin
in his leather pouch; or impatiently waving you on.

And when you learned he'd passed, you thought of the other man
working the Antill lights, further up. Adjacent to the TAB,
which he'd regularly shuffle across to in his thongs.
Did the pair know each other?; and, if so, ever associate?
Or is squeegeeing, like the trade of light-keepers,
a more solitary task—with no real opportunity of meeting
in the natural course of your work.

Each man tending his separate post
on the other side of our windscreens. Day and night, for years.
With the same long, exposed stretch of avenue
connecting them through the seasons,
two kilometres apart on the long, broad straight.

Us always looking out at them, and they only ever incidentally
looking sidewards and in.
Before, with their curt work done (either compensated
or uncompensated, and with our glass dramatically the better
for their squeegees' attention or not),
we slid our vehicles back into gear with the light change,
to accelerate our way off and on.

Trompe l'oeil: miracle off Northbourne

A woman crosses Northbourne at the lights,
dressed in flouncy, tangerine-coloured skirt,
white-lace blouse buttoned high at the throat,
and chunky bright, white running-shoes.
Pushing a gleaming-new chrome wheelchair before her:
one white whippet sat erect within it,
and another tripping nimbly on a leash behind.

Your eyes drink this beguiling sight in,
like some miracle you weren't privileged to actually see:
just glimpsing this taunting aftermath
of the grandly accomplished thing ...
Some event taken place off-scene
(just a block back say, in East Row—
on Petrie or Akuna Street).
And referencing themes (tropes, memes) of Lameness,
Samaritan-style Compassion, or Providence,
entangled a pair of slender, white coursing dogs ...

As this troupe now processes its way off
on slick, silver wheels, chunky white rubber heels
and nimbly flicked paws.
Bearing itself proud, erect and tall, purposeful and trim—
cutting westward, along Alinga Street.

A fine-dressed, upright, Christian woman
pushing a gleaming-new wheelchair before her.
One whippet sat royally upright within it,
and a second trotting briskly at heel, behind.

Ecology

(Mulligans Flat Nature Reserve, Gungahlin)

> *'Reintroduction programs are planned for animals not sighted in the Canberra region for over a century'*

To rehabilitate the woodland Reserve
of tussock grass, yellow box and Blakely's red gum,
they first reintroduced the Eastern Bettong,
a rabbit-sized kangaroo and 'ecosystem engineer'
—to aerate the soil, and disperse seed and spore.

Then followed this up with the Native Mouse,
though (in a sort of ecological 'confidentiality clause')
not disclosing this as projected prey
for forthcoming release (return)
of the Spot-Tailed Quoll, or 'Tiger Cat'.
To serve as apex predator of the food chain,
and consummate full rehabilitation of the place.

But this scheme, alas, like those of all native New Holland
mice and men, suffered setback one night
when protesters against the kangaroo cull
cut 30 holes in the 2-metre-high mesh
of the Reserve's 12-kilometre-long,
cat-fox-&-dog-proof perimeter fence.

Gang-gang

(Emblem bird of the ACT)

Evolution had a bad hair day
the day it crafted you.
Trying for the Galah some say,
but only part way there by the shift's end,
and setting you aside on the workbench
to start anew.

Meantime, wily you,
inveigled yourself clean away.
But that's all spilt milk now.
And despite your undeniable shortcomings
and prototypic state—
poor finish and raggedy style:
your blighted, unkempt topknot,
untuned *grek-groke* call
and cockamamie, Marty-Feldman eye—
you're quite endearing (or at least compelling)
in your individual way.
We've grown quite attached to you,
and care for you as much as the galah
(some even *more*), today.
And declare you fully fit for service
in our *Big Book of Australian Birds* for sure.

Lament: the lake, the reef

Burley Griffin's soft corals are patently stressed,
its biodiversity diminishing by the day—
as attested by a recent lunchtime walk
from King's to Commonwealth Bridge
which failed to locate endemic populations
of butterfly, angel, clown, or orange-finned anemone fish.
Sea cucumbers and cuttles likewise appeared
in unabashed retreat. (Though miraculously somehow
the brave carp clings on
by trembling, rosy finger-tips.)

Now, while we might squander ill-affordable time
debating the causes for such decline
(depredation by introduced-species;
diversion of waters upstream;
the colossal ecological folly
of the Captain Cook Memorial Fountain;
or bank erosion by scullers from AIS)—
immediate intervention is imperative
to ensure this unique environment is not lost to us forever.
In like manner to the destruction of the Great Manuka Marshlands
and the Swinger Hill Savannah. The river red gum forests
which once graced Garema Place. And the decimation of
the dugong populations which, within the present writer's memory,
frolicked in wanton abandon and profusion on the ANU campus,
all along the seagrass-strewn reaches of Sullivan's Creek.

Captain Cook Memorial Water Jet Variations

1. Saturation (the pedal-boat)

Perpetual-toppling waterspout.
Rainbow's manufactory.
Angel's wing: sky-pierced,
and lit through sheer as negligee;
clinging to the great silvery weft of yourself
in all your haughty, dazzling allure—

though the gazetteer has Belize or Borneo
as the wettest place on earth,
I know in fact that place is here:

sitting in this pedal-boat,
parked right under you.

2. Runaway (Après toi, le déluge?)

Most days your drop-zone is the size of a squash court,
or fit space in which a chamber orchestra
might comfortably seat itself to play.
But when an ill wind blows,
you fumble a dark hand inside yourself:
turn rogue, explode, and jump the fence!
To billow in a raging spinnaker,
and attain your most damaging reach.

You constitute a public menace then.
Ensnaring Commonwealth Bridge in your driftnet.
Scattering pedestrians, obliging good, honest and hard-working
public servants to smartly lift their feet.
Cyclists hunch, and pedal hard
to toboggan their way through.
Cars' windscreen-wiper blades machete frantically
at the inordinate thicket of you ...
And, short of some providential easing of the wind,
no means exists of taming or containing you at all:
barring a call to Municipal Services
to switch your machinery off.

3. Fantasy: the waterspout, the carp, the Parliament

One night I dreamt you uprooted yourself
from your Regatta Point mooring post,
and sucking all the lake's carp-stock aboard,
drifted like a waterspout
the full course of Commonwealth Avenue,
to arrive over Capitol Hill.
Then broke in a peremptory thunderclap:
disgorging your entire fish-load,
crashing through Parliament's roof
to flop glass-eyed and gasping on the chamber floor.

At this (in a rare show of bipartisan support)
they called in the ADF, to throw all means of ordinance your way
in an attempt to neutralise you.
Like those monstrous sci-fi ants in the Fifties cult-film *Them!*

But, for all this show of fulsome and gung-ho macho,
they'd still not got your measure by the time that I awoke ...
Though via another dreamer I learned
they'd eventually run you down to some bolthole motel
just outside Yass. And, under full military escort
of Bushmaster protected mobility vehicles
flanked by Abrams tanks,
had dragged you back to the capital triumphantly in chains.
And bolted you more securely to your post,
to resume your fit-and-proper service in the lake.

Rowing Song
(Lake Burley Griffin)

Eights training

Gently shouldering their craft, like an angel's wing
in plaster-cast, they bear it to the water's edge,
swing it down, then topple themselves in:
to sit thigh-deep, entrenched within its slippery tightrope
like a slim-line billycart.

Each spends a private moment sorting out
the awkward business of his oar,
before straightening to face the runtish cox.
A gang of big, athletic fellows,
looking frankly ridiculous
in so insufficient a vehicle
for the comfortable ferrying of eight full-grown men,
plus a littler one plomped in at one end to watch.
Then lean, to put their big, collective
shoulder to the wheel—dig their blades tips hard in
and, in singleted unison, kick off!
Commencing to manhaul themselves.
Abseiling upriver ...

Pretty soon they're right into their stroke.
Winching themselves (taut-tricepped, bull-necked,
bent backs) like a route march cut off at the hip—
settling to a steady lope, to make their deft ingress
with admirable finesse, and grace.
Stepping out twin-tracks of nippled water,
which ripple further out like swollen areola ...

Manhandled thus, their vessel jerks forward by increments:

                                                                 A-
                            gain.

                                      A-
           gain.

                             A-
gain ...

Now, hurtling toward the course's end,
this may look peachy and silk-smooth to us
stood on the bank. But doubtless there, at ground zero
(in the driver's seat, and engine-room)
it hurts like hell in arm, shoulder, chest
and sacroiliac ... Until eventually, skedaddled in,
their craft coasts to a halt.
Their big, sleek-lean muscle-machine coming undone.
The rowers broken to a man, scattered oars in disarray,
heads bowed between splayed knees:
their craft a poor, pale, cringing, stump-tailed thing—
limped its fraught, weary way in
to willow-weeping home.

Postscript: the coxswain's story

And where, in this,
was their little stern task-master, the cox?
Seeming content to sit, arms crossed
and hugging himself. Capped head barely level
with their sveltely heaving chests,
in his sedan-chair up the back.
Glancing idly off as all the world is hurtling past
on blades' tiptoes; the riverbank in a blind rush.

As if waiting to be peeled a grape, almost.
Or with the air of a concussed jockey,
tossed from his mount in a steeplechase.

Sweet Christ, was ever such a sinecure
contrived in the history of sport?
That consummate freeloader
just couldn't lift an oar to save himself,
as they propel themselves and his deadweight home.

Sacrificials 1 & 2

1. The dying place

This tame-looking lake can be a killing-place:
in addition to the tourists,
murder, suicide and accident visit its waters too.

On occasion, people have fallen to drown
in its chill, still, narrow waters
from their canoe.

A youth jumped from Commonwealth Bridge
one winter night.
(Despite the lake's modest depth,
it took a week of dragging
for his body to be retrieved by police boat.)

And on the West Basin's shore,
toward the Heritage Nursery,
a jogger found the body of a young woman,
last seen buying cigarettes from her local hotel
a few weeks before.
Her naked body lashed to a concrete bolster,
and cicatrised with knife-wounds.
(Police following a lead she'd been driven there
by a perpetrator in a black ute.)

These and other present-day propitiations
could be construed as 'sacrifices' of a kind.
Here under these skies, in this lake with its quicksilver changes
from cement-grey, through deep violet,
to mirror-clear, cirrusy azure.

Even though such suffering, desperation and pain
never formed any intended, inherent (coherent) part
of Griffin's vision or 'The Plan'
whatsoever, you'd presume.

2. *All the pretty, drowned horses*

A *Canberra Times* article tells
that to create the West Basin,
part of the Royal Canberra Golf Course
and some cricket grounds (located on private grazing land
from which livestock were required to be dispersed
prior to commencement of a game)
were resumed. Out there, near where
a remnant part of the drowned property 'Springbank'
is preserved in a small, barrow-shaped island
of the same name.

And that, in further pursuit of Griffin's plan
commanding that the free-running river 'Molonglo'
be flooded, to create the lake—
all the pretty, galloping horses in their bright racing colours
were strangled and drowned out there
on their dusty racing-track too.

'Rusty'

(Anzac Day, Australian War Memorial)

This massive thing
compacted down to this small,
token animal—
led tripping in by halter and rein
on slim fetlocks
from Anzac Avenue.

Saddle stripped,
riding boots reversed in the stirrups.
The entire First AIF set there,
upon this horse called 'Rusty'.
Who, the commentator says,
following his long period of service
will be retired from duty this year.

And another horse broken
to fit his place.

The *1812* on Anzac Parade

> *'My little piece may not be remembered, but it will be loud'*
> *(Tchaikovsky)*

Other neighbourhoods contend with hoons in cars,
torched wheelie-bins or over-enthused partiers—
but here, 200 years on from Napoleon's retreat,
Campbell brunts the *Overture*.
As the ADF's six field howitzers
(in synch with high-kicking fireworks,
and digital cathedral bells)
each detonate emphatically in turn ...
Echoing the length of the Parade:
triggering a car alarm in Blamey Crescent
and frightening sweet bejeezus out of someone's hound.
As Australia's Federation Guard perseveres uncowed,
with weapons shouldered,
in a drifting pall which mingles cannon smoke and fireworks.
In a raking enfilade of autumn rain.

Papuan post-figures

('Sentani double-figure', National Gallery of Australia)

These twin figures seem to float:
slender, knock-kneed creatures
with jutting chins and wasted arms,
shrunken monkey-buttocks.
Joined at the hip, and slightly turned out from each other
in their dark, lichen-etched wood.
Like two stiff spirit-birds perched
on a great Ghost-Ancestor's shoulder.
The expression of the blank, ellipsoidal discs
of their uptilted faces
either consummately stupid,
or obliterated with all-knowing.
As they drift, weightless as waterlilies,
being eaten up into air.

What is their mission or purpose?
Where might they be tripping to,
forever locked there, together-and-alone.
Are they Husband-&-Wife?
Mother-&-Son? Brother-&Sister?
No curator knows—but they are contrived
from a very hard wood, we are told,
hewn with great persistence by an adze of stone.

Dredged up from the lake into which they had either haphazardly fallen,
or been jettisoned on arrival of the missionaries decades ago,
these carved post-figures from a remote fishing village in Papua
artlessly seduce you into their wild, wistful,
unknowable, gravity-free realm.
Have you utterly hooked.

Vale, National Tally Room

(Budawang Building, Exhibition Park)

In the Electoral Commission's big triennial fit-out,
the yawing barn of the Budawang Building
(other-time venue of the Lifeline Book Fair
and ski-wear and Persian rug sales)
thrummed like the bullpen of a stock market floor.
Its big tally-board revealing the full, gerrymandered jigsaw
of Australia in its electoral parts,
as commentators scried their laptops' crystal balls
in the broadcasters booths in front.
(One interviewing a bull-faced candidate
who sweated like he just might lose.)

When we'd eventually had our fill
and drifted back out to the night parking lot,
the harness-race training was continuing at the track next door.

> Under ET-grade arc-lights a lone, hobbled horse
> was trying its best to lift its feet in its tangled drawers,
> inspired by the driver's lashing its rump
> in aid of the cause.
> The Cross tilted awry overhead,
> and at that point of the count at least,
> the Parliament appeared to be hung.
> With odds on that, as sure as that poor horse was struggling,
> the interviewed candidate was dead in his seat.

Mexican wave

(Australia-Italy Rugby Test, Bruce Stadium, June 2009)

Two false starts and it's finally away:
wobbling a little unevenly at first
like a buckled bicycle wheel.
     Building its wonky momentum
in an anticlockwise steeplechase
of erupting polystyrene coffee cups,
match programs, beanies and scarves
all sent spiracling up into the Canberra night air ...
Tiptoeing one wowser crowd-stretch
to reignite itself: crackling like wildfire,
building momentum again.

A few distracted Wallabies glance out sidewards
from the steaming, packed muscle-mass of the scrum.
An Italian flanker goofily smiles—
as, now really letting it have its head
     (*Ole*! *Yee-hah! Banzai*!)
the crowd brings the thing galloping, teetering and careening
round raggedly again ... Then again, and again,
for eight circuits straight, three heroic minutes in all.
Till eventually faltering, grown weary of itself,
it sinks down on one knee, drops onto an elbow
and then finally falls flat on its face.
To disappear through a hole-in-the-crowd
in the Gregan-Larkham stand
from whence it came.

This fine, irreverent thing.
The crowd's bastard child and bit of wanton *braggadocio*
contrived to warm and cheer itself
on a piercing-cold June night.
(In a frankly moribund game.)

Then left to hibernate there, stored deep in the stadium's muscle.
Till it gets its recall and is pulled off the bench
some subsequent, suitable day and game.

Aquarium songs

(National Zoo & Aquarium, Yarralumla)

Freshwater species ('Riverland')

At Scrivener Dam the haltered lake
Houdinis through the concrete spill-wall,
before reorienting itself
to become 'Molonglo' again.
And samples of our native fish-stock
silently parade themselves
       slim-hipped and dour-mouthed
       (showing off—'Look Ma, no hands!')
through corridors of wrist-thick plexiglass
in the watery-walled cathedral-world of 'Riverland'.
Swim tirelessly round,
              and round,
                            and round
       (again
              again
                            again):

Sooty Grunter,
                        Spotted Scat,
       Saratoga,
                        Spangled Perch
      Mangrove Jack   and more.
Each trailing the magic incantation of their name.

Murray Cod

In the Cafeteria, a Murray Cod
the size of a bloated dog
or shell of a Great War howitzer
bobs in its feature tank,
watching on like a demented waiter as we eat.

Sixty years of age; weight a hundred kilograms.
Close-up, you can see a jagged scar
like the healed tear in a boxer's lip
which shows where it was hooked—
as it hovers, hobbled there. Looking winded:
like the whole of Burley Griffin
had its front wheels parked on its chest.
All imagination crushed from it,
its grey, gaping hell-mouth a garage door
to a whole, awful Otherworld ...

Adrift like a crippled spacecraft.
Or like Laika, imprisoned in the *Sputnik*,
as we lament not having the technology
to ever bring her home.

Marine species

This pair shanghaied to here,
three hours inland from their native, saltwater home.
Hung abreast, in their song of separateness,
conspiring together-and-alone
                as light wafts down
                      like soggy benediction,
to crown their lumpen heads.

        'Hump-headed Maori Wrasse',
        & 'Speckled Grouper'.

Glassy-eyed, expressionless,
as they gravitate sidelong,
performing tidy three-point turns
deftly as forklifts.

Suspended there: on call
to somehow come into themselves.
Hovering like some Dream-Team second-row,
waiting to pack down and screw the scrum
or entire axis of this Earth—*forever*.

Cupcake

(Fyshwick Markets)

The child kneels at the Bakery's glass case, to consider the array
of the green, froggy-face cupcake with Smarties smile and eyes;
the marshmallow one with thick-chocolate icing that splodges
the end of your nose; and the yummy-squidgy custardy one
she had once before on her brother's birthday.
As the shoppers huddle behind the police tape.
And her mother stands riven with remorse, for ever having brought
her child into this world, to face just such a calamitous choice as this.
And the child herself, even at her tender age, intuits that this act is critical.
With not the remotest margin for mistake—no chance for fall-back
or to recant, at all. There can be victory for only one *törtchen*
here today. As her finger staggers toward the glass.
To rule on this whole, dire, murderous matter once-and-for-all.
And nominate the correct cupcake.

Getting the drift

(Canberra Balloon Fiesta, Parliamentary Triangle)

Gross-bloated festoons of colour
writ themselves large-and-round,
loud-and-proud in big capital letters,
to brazenly promote themselves in the billboard sky.

Talked themselves up to head-butt it at their various heights.
Blooming like gaudy, cartoon flak
released from Black Mountain's loopy imagining,
as they totter-and-mill above us awhile.
Like a posse vaguely intent on heading off in due time,
should some suitable quarry or purpose
be identified or defined—
but meanwhile just enjoying the view.
Hanging round, feeling the sun on their backs
and making their balloon-hay while it shines.

Good-natured, buoyant and bountiful,
expecting the very best from Life.
Having hung themselves up in blind faith,
anticipating no enemies: no lightning bolt to rudely dislodge them
from their big faithful blue friend The Sky.
Feeling so incredibly full of themselves,
though of course it's just all that hot-air they sheathe,
which keeps them flying high.
Suspended where they are:

                there

   there

                         there

                                  there

       THERE ...

As they now commence their rotund cakewalk,
dragged slowly side-wise downwind.
Trundling in loose convoy. Getting the drift of this world,
lackadaisically ferried to the near-ends of the sky ...

Till eventually their big party's picked slowly undone—
and the earth calls each in, one-by-one,
dragged remorselessly down to the lumbering ground.
Then duly collapses, folds and empties them
and stuffs them all back into their big wicker baskets
and they die.

Ode to *Skywhale*

(Canberra Centenary celebrations, 2013)

Great-tottering, rat-fucked *Hindenburg*,
        nightmare kiddy-jumping-castle—
your bovine armament like bunker-busting cantaloupes,
slung giddily off each wing—What twisted vision created,
then (more alarmingly) unleashed you,
to perpetrate this outrage on our home skies?

What bastard mission were you assigned,
by what pox-brained Admiralty, to venture so high?
Squinnying down sidewards on us
with your warty, reptile eye. Belly-scraping our lake's tranquil waters
to terrify twelve varieties of tripe from its innocent carp?

Apoplectic archangel,
        beast of some strange, cockamamie Apocalypse—
what smoky, backroom cluster-fuck of miscegenation
bred you? What might you denote, or connote,
as you stomp your pirate-faced way about.
(Vouchsafed, we hear tell, your own Twitter account,
for putting your eerie messages out
with the midnight trash, like Trump's.)

Heinous, shameless, abominable, rotund dirigible—
        sow-teated pumpkin-stormcloud—
you have tarried too long, divided opinion too much!
Time to sort your manifold, slippery-tangled dugs out
and hoist them aboard. Disengage our tidy foreshore,
and point your nose south, for Melbourne.
(Your evident new home, despite we ACT-ratepayers
having been suckered into footing your bill.)

Adieu then, *Skywhale*. Too-roo! You were too hot to handle it's true.
The mere notion of you was perhaps ill-judged,
you should have just died on the drawing board.
In any case it's safe bet that the Territory will think thrice,
and opt for something more sanguine of design—
more safe, and vastly less 'in-your-face'—
when the Bi-Centenary swings round. For sure.

King parrots' descent

In Spring's sweet motorcade, the three fruit trees—
apple, apricot and pear—arrayed at our back fence
have dropped their crimson-white flowers
like tickertape ... As a King parrot pair,
leaving off the chiacking and malarkey
of their high-wire shenanigans, swing down
onto the apple's upper branch. Face off from its opposite ends,
then ape-walk toward each other, fist-over-beak-over-hand,
to meet and playfully bump heads.
Brazenly canoodle there, in their savage, spraycan orange
and two-tone green.
Their cries—two taut-and-perfect, peeling bells—
cutting my tame-and-flabby heart like razor-wire
to its core's quick.

Two elegies

Bringing down the gum

(Eucalyptus blakelyi, Selwyn Street)

Century-old gum, it was hard when the freak October gust
found you out: sending two large branches crashing down
to shatter diagonally across the road.
More so when, in the aftermath, the tree surgeon diagnosed
the fatal crack running lengthwise up your trunk,
obliging us to bring down the rest of you as well.

That said, in their butchering the chainsaws
served you as nobly as they could.
Trimming you into chunky, artful parts.
Most of which we gave away to friends as firewood.
But a sample selection we retained, commemorating you.
Showcasing aspects of your grain,
or lovely, silky, mottled soft-and-dark-grey bark.

> Branch sections shaped like plump, rolled,
> hotel bathroom towels;
> blocky stumps cut square as a marine's haircut.
> And sundry other odd off-cuts
> for the possible making up
> of picture frames or cutting-boards.
> Keepsakes to remember you by.

Including six larger blocks cut from the main trunk,
bum-beckoning as milking-stools,
which we arranged in an impromptu circle in our front yard.
Where they stand glistening in the autumn rain
as I look through our lounge window now,
and delight in the rich-lacquered Kimberley earth-tone
which erupts, tumbling out of you.
And come at last to profoundly grasp
the true sense of your name: ... Red Gum.

The cleansing

(Mount Majura)

Dropped in your crumpled hide-and-bone,
in the khaki-coloured grass on the hill, beside the fire-trail—
your muzzle was a shrunken purse
of blanched teeth and slender mandible;
your deer-like face collapsed, and laughing bitterly into itself—
the silky-red leather of your belly bereft of fur,
but your big tail still full and whole. Extended emphatically out
with the resounding power of a bull-whip's crack:
game and powerful as an old boxer's arm
over all the trashed, wasted else ...

And you reminded me of that other big male
(stood eye-to-eye with me, when reared on its toes)
which hard times had brought down
from the neighbouring reserve to sprawl sleepy-eyed on its side
under the front-yard wattle, years ago.
And inclined to browse the nursery-bought native grass, Pennstripe,
which I'd planted in the dug-up lawn.
(Its diligent nibbling seeming to endorse that grass choice.)

A regular visitant, right up until,
concerned for the kids' safety in their games,
and after seeking Municipal Services advice,
I dusted its resting site with Brunnings Blood-&-Bone
to nudge it safely on.
                              (This worked.)

Bush news

(Mount Majura)

Mount Majura prayer: Summer

Halfway up the trail
to the dry waterfall
you can sit on stone steps
and look through a gap in the trees
down onto the plain below,
to see all of Civic suspended there.

Its pet huddle of buildings laid low
in the summer heat:
so neat, small and square
that you could hold it whole,
like water cupped in both hands.

Before clambering back to your feet, refreshed,
with the strength to carry your way on again.

Cockatoo evening

Look up!
      The cockatoos wing raucously about,
like surging white caps, that cross /
    recross
          the neighbourhood.

Raffish and rag-tag, purely out to enjoy themselves.
      Croaking their rude pleas
as they drag themselves about the sky in gay discord,
like tin cans tied behind the wedding car …

Until each, by wayward fits-and-turns
(in its own easy time,
according to personal whim, style and mood)
has eventually wended its way home.

To garage itself in its night haunt
in the dark pines by Hackett playing fields.

Lester Young plays the Top Dam

(Mount Majura Nature Reserve with Walkman)

I saw Lester Young play the Top Dam.
Stood in his crumpled Brooks Brothers suit,
wearing his winsome frown.
Wingtip shoes sunk in the muddy bank.
Lotus-lid eyes slit to a dreamy close,
pork pie hat slid back on his head
as he blew his sweet chops.
Sax angled out sidewards in that signature pose
like a feminine side-saddle almost;
or a shag's bent wing, hung out to ventilate …

Kicking on, in that sweet-limpid, spare swing
of pure, drop-dead deliciousness …
as an echidna shuffled its way by
through leaf-litter on the walking track,
entirely disarmed. And a roo sidled in dam-side—to crouch,
stretch its neck out and timorously drink,
plump joey juggling itself in her pouch …

And two waterbirds sat hunched,
each on a separate branch of a big, toppled gum.
An egret, and a cormorant, both the approximate size
of a tenor saxophone's bell.
Perched like hepcats, tuned to the Prez's groove.
Listening there, together-and-alone
like a pair of feathered misanthropes,
each fixed in their own bird-spacetime realm.

As if Life had become way too complicated these days
for two different species of waterbird to commune,
or to share the same branch of one tree in this world …

As dam-side meanwhile,
Lester for his part played sweetly on.

CAPITAL & REGIONAL CONUNDRUMS

Canberra: A defence

Most of us are pretty well detached
from the ongoing, suited-bloodsport on the hill.
And this city is as random a mix
of the enchanting and mediocre,
banal and broad-spectrum criminal,
as your own cities are for the rest of you.

Though on balance you'd say,
that with its human scale and quiet bushscape,
it's a fine place overall in which to live, work
and raise your kids. The four seasons, and easy reach
of both sea and snow appeal.
And there's little mystery:
we like living here, we really do.
     (More so since IKEA and Costco
     have both recently come to town too.)

Gridlock arrives in the Capital

(2006)

The Bush Capital's muscled up
and we've got our own peak-hour now:
which didn't exist on our arrival here
back a decade ago.

Now, if we could just convince the Prime Minister
to move from Sydney's North Shore
and live here in town as we do:
he could enjoy a taste of the Capital's
new impressive, big-city-style gridlock too!

The flag ('Summer Holiday'?)

(New Parliament House)

Parliament's flag is 'as big as a double-decker bus',
the Tourist Authority tells.
Well sure, okay—but with the nation's bus
being driven precisely where to?

> Belconnen Mall?
> On Cliff Richard's 'Summer Holiday'?
> Or cartwheeling head-over-tail,
> all the way down the giddy, slippery slope
> to Mediocrity, Perdition & Hell?

Song: Spring-thing

(From the National Library)

Poplar fluff in the UN's ornamental pool
is stirred to a thick béarnaise,
as a Municipal Services groundsman breaks pretty rainbows,
steam-hosing the most intimate parts
of the Henry Moore.
(*Two-Piece Reclining Figure No. 9.*)
And, across on the lake's far side
a distant freeman walks, with head bowed,
along the Nerang Pool wall.
Treading a tightrope of pure, liquid light
(and whistling maybe, who knows,
Hey-nonny-noh! for all he's worth) ...

As the capital pushes its big, mad, bad, dangerous beauty at us,
all around.
And the High Court, astride its Brutal-concrete high-horse,
keeps intent watch.
As if asked to adjudicate on this whole, unruly Spring-thing,
and determine the constitutionality of it all.

Mitchell's Cure (Or 'So long and thanks for all the fish'): A true story
(for BM)

The carp are a plague and pestilence
with no immediate, compelling cure—
though our neighbour Bill's quietly onto it,
in his tinnie with 2-horsepower Evinrude.

Diligently hooking and landing the things,
giving each a wallop on the head,
then renditioning them to his Downer backyard.
To play bottom-feeders of a sort again:

swimming a half-metre underground,
fertilising his dahlia bed.

Lament: The servos

Anywhere else in this wide world,
they'd live free alongside the main roads,
but in *this* town any you somehow manage to find
will be tucked away down some ill-lit backstreet,
as if ashamed of disclosing themselves ...

As if filling your tank were some discreet, private act
akin to toileting yourself.

Or the bowsers were licensed to just come out at night
and ringing their bells aloud,
to spare us sight of their blighted stumps and sores.

The bunnies

While a semi-detached in Madigan
flogs 'pedigree Dutch Silk Dwarf' baby rabbits
at $10 each,

Parks & Wildlife's busy gassing bunnies en masse in their burrows,
in the Reserve 300 metres up the street.

Summernats redemption
(Or: 'Hey, we do hoon *here*, too!')

(First week of January, EPIC, Mitchell)

Might the sense of vented fury-&-rage
infecting our north Canberra houses and yards
in the first week of every January
(to induce the fight-or-flight reflex in me)

be assuaged, if the over-torqued Summernats crowd
could just avail themselves
of the 6 am Yoga-Meditation sessions
which the Folk Festival offers at that same venue,
in the Easter of every year?

Hibernation

(late Autumn, Gilbert Street)

Winter is icumen in,
oak leaves tumble the length of our street:

under its custom-cut, polytarp cover
next door's putting their Blue Haven pool to sleep.

Painting the elephant

(Nimmitabel, the Monaro)

To protect it from High Country heat and frosts
they paint the Balinese elephant
in Dulux Weathershield.

A pastel peach-pink
(number 39 in the 'Heritage Range'):
to tone in with all the other Heritage monuments
of the town's main street, I guess.

Wetsuit: the corrections

(Lines to a young surfer at Broulee)

Broad-shouldered, strong and able as you seem,
stood square-footed in your wet-suit's snug fit—
just remember this, young gun:

if a Great White should happen on you out there,
you're just a poorer, paler cut
of seal-meat to it.

> *(Think on this Grasshopper, my son.*
> *Please think on this.)*

OVER THE MOUNTAINS TO THE SEA

Two takes on Weereewa

Weereewa (aka 'George')

The lake called 'George' (or 'Weereewa',
in its native Ngunnawal)
hardly makes a lake at all:
any more than a shaken snow-dome
constitutes a real snowstorm.

And though on passing it today
the skies are grey, and its parched bed taunts:
still, through no true (directly attributable) fault of its own,
no water falls into the lake
called Weereewa (or George) at all.

With most likely none in fact to fall
tomorrow, or this week—
for the whole of the remaining year
and maybe even five years more. (Who knows?
It's El Nino's, or La Nina's, call.)

As the lake sits pat, in its ancient fault-bones,
obliging you each time you pass
to just take it on face; embrace it as the season comes.
Accept it all with gratitude and grace
(or resignation at last call).
And play this landscape as it falls.

For—whether a sheep-keeping place,
a grass-floored reservoir,
or some messed-up, quagmiry No Man's Land
parked somewhere in between—
nonetheless by name it will remain:
Weereewa. (Or 'Lake George'.)

Though certainly you'd have to say
that hauling past the thing today,
no water whatsoever shows
in this paddock, lake or meta-lake
(called George or 'Weereewa'—whatever):
Nix, *niente*, *nada*, *zilch*. Sweet bugger-all.

Double-take: Chaplin encounters 'King' Yates on Lake George

The 'Little Fellow' sits, insouciant, at a camping table on the baked claypan. Kohl-ringed eyes, bowler hat and cane. White shirt shucked off and laid as tablecloth as he feasts upon his boiled, left boot. Lifts a glass of water, sips—then frowns as something suddenly erupts into the middle distance, then hurtles past flat-chat: 'King' Yates, in racing goggles and leather pilot's cap. Bent prostrate over the tank of his motorbike.

Upon the pass, both men do classic Vaudeville double-takes. The speedster intrigued to see such epicurean feat executed in so unlikely and insalubrious a place. (Relieved, on top, to find the table not directly set in his speed's way.) And the Little Fellow to observe (appreciate) how efficiently Yates and his machine could accelerate, to dervish clear from view.

Then, cocking his head manfully to left, then right, as the dust-drift settles on his plate and stings his round, brown childlike blinking eyes—and wriggling both buttocks for improved purchase of his stool—Chaplin re-commandeers his knife and fork, wings both pinkies out, and soulfully resumes his booty meal ... While Yates and motorbike, as just dessert, proceed to set a new land-speed record.

HIGH COUNTRY

The Snowy also rises. (The pollinators)

Sprung from Ram's Head's granite pyramid,
the river's just a hand-span wide
as it commences plaiting its way down
through sphagnum bog.
Gathering gravity and consequence
as it fossicks the hillside—
finding the simplest line-of-fall.
Divining its true nature,
building direction and form.
Sorting itself out by sudden sweet
swoops,
                twists
    and rills.
With brief pauses at wayside pools—
before cutting a metre-wide swathe through heathland,
and elbowing past a knee-high Plum Pine
which hugs a rock as windbreak.

    This tree is 800 years old,
    and its berries a delicacy
    for the mountain pigmy possum, the ranger tells,
    indicating the signature scat alongside.

    Ravens are the only birds you'll find
    above the tree-line. It's too high for bees as well,
    and the March flies are vital as pollinators up here.
    So we'll just have to put up with their bites, she
    says—

leaving us to plod our way on alone
up to the metal catwalk, toward the summit ridge.

Instructions for walking mountain country
(Or: The mountain rules OK. Respect!)

Lightning strikes are the norm up here,
an essential and vital part of the ecological flux,
kick-starting hundreds of scrub fires each year—
usually just burning out, though a few dramatically take.
And lightning *is* something to think about,
treading this long, clattering catwalk of raised metal-plate
brazenly baring its teeth to the open sky
like a kilometre-long lightning-rod clamped to your feet.
And remembering the park ranger's cautionary tale
of the woman hiker struck in her bra's under-wire
and hospitalised for a year with third-degree burns to her chest.

Yes, the weather looms large up here
in the Park's big, dangerous backyard:
a deep, incontrovertible, permanent presence
in this freehold of tor, heath, tarn and scree,
glacial lake and moraine. Cleft deep in the hard,
granite scheme-of-things. You need to watch your back:
wind, rain, snow and sleet can sidle in over this landscape in a blink.
Always carry adequate gear, as much for a day-walk
as a week-long trek. Be careless—move off-track,
and try jay-walking up here, and the mountain will run you down.
The weather can turn on a misty whim; in a heartbeat
(though to use the word 'treacherous' as some do
is absurd: when it's simply a matter of the mountain
keeping true to the word of itself, and its spirit-of-place).

Be sensible, discreet. *You* are the potential transgressor up here:
the superfluous (superficial), intervening 'foreign' thing.
If you reckon you can outfox the wily old mountain
then just refer to the record of all those who didn't,
and became stranded in mist, pall, drift or blizzard.
Who the mountain struck down mercilessly
over the years: ranging from the pioneer stockmen,

through Laurie Seaman (in whose memory the emergency-hut was built)—
on up to the young city snowboarders last season.
>   Warned by Parks staff not to venture onto the mountain that day.
>   And pulled rigid in their frozen sleeping bags
>   from their collapsed snowcave
>   when the thaw ate them out of their burrow the following spring.

The mountain rules. Always, okay. *Respect*!

Kosciuszko Report

(Mt Kosciuszko: 2,228 metres; 7,310 feet)

And today on the mountain, breaking news is:
that some maverick's holed himself up in Seaman's Hut
to charge passing hikers admission.
Now, with his threat to start killing people,
Parks staff have called in the Jindabyne police.

> (You imagine a pair of them sharing a chairlift up.
> Sat side-by-side: black dangling boots,
> Smith & Wessons bulging on hips,
> close-shaven cheeks pinked-up in the brisk mountain air.
> Framed there, floating against the sky:
> blue-against-blue; The Sky/The Police …
> Then riding their chair-posse back down
> with their man cuffed, and sat either across their laps
> or jammed in tight on the seat in between.
> But they drive the paddy-van up
> along the Charlotte's Pass fire-trail instead.)

It's the topic of conversation up here,
as we watch on from the summit cairn.
Fifty-odd sunburned mums-dads-&-kids
sipping bottled spring water, and picnicking on
health bars and sandwiches. Sat on this rocky slope
as if awaiting the trick with the loaves-&-fish.
As the van reappears: limping its way gingerly back down
through the shattered crockery of the scree,
like a man being frogmarched with wrists bound behind
and being mindful not to slip.
Slowly feeling its way down from these granite heights
like the Snowy River itself.

So: The Mounties have got their man
and Kosciuszko can breathe free again,
we think to ourselves, observing this.
Feeling high, and a little vertiginous,
in our big box-seat up here.
Taking the air on our serviceable peak,

at just a quarter the height of Everest.
As the spring sun pours beneficently down on Australia's roof.
And our hearts tremble and swell like an auditorium's floorboards
resounding under the collective rattle-thump-&-stomp
of all the mountain's 73-hundred feet.

Bushfire season: the comedians

(Kiandra Road, Kosciusko National Park)

The bush-brigade loll against their truck
and hug themselves in folded arms
in their butter-yellow fire-suits,
as they coolly watch the slow-burning red line
      tippling upward,
                      right-to-left.
Like an artful sketch in poured napalm,
tiptoeing the heath-ridge towards them.

Calmly measuring it, as it's maybe measuring them:
burning small and modest for now,
if perhaps with designs of improving itself.
Appeaseable, contained: smouldering quite homely at this distance,
like a peat-cake in the hearth.
Something which might amicably turn itself in,
or just quietly burn itself out, as they watch on.

They're awaiting the brigade captain's call
from his command post up the road.
It's a fine art, judging fires. Knowing when to kit-up
and baton-charge, taking it on.
And when to jump into the cabin, to cut-and-run.
Timing is everything: fire-fighters are comedians
who can burn in their trucks if the gag goes wrong.

Still, for now the crew is content to just linger and watch,
as the thin red line now commences slowly piddling its way down
a gentle incline some three hundred metres off.
Flames being idly dropped from its pockets,
quite flagrantly enjoying itself on its big day out.
Just like the fire-fighters themselves:
now shrugged their yellow jackets off
and stood smiling in navy blue T-shirts.
Sipping tea from enamel mugs and yarning in the pleasant spring sun,
as the fire ankle-bites its way across the heath towards them.

Daytrip to the snowfield

(Mount Selwyn)

The Snowy Scheme's mass-planted poplars and willows waltz us across the bald heath. High-voltage powerlines Godzilla their way across too: stomping, with elbows akimbo, crossing the highway right and left. And on reaching the Park gates we discover a good snowfall—for the first time in our lives having to fit chains to our car wheels. (Ingénues, clumsily fumbling them on; myself supplying the muscle, my wife the fine-motor skills.)

Smiggins Hole is closed by a blizzard, but the Mount Selwyn road is clear—and halfway there we pull in at a wood-slab hut constructed a century ago. Eucalypt table, benches, and a welcoming hearth with the remains of a log fire obligingly left simmering still. Which we heap up to keep us company, with our fruit cake and thermos tea.

A snowplough chuffs by during this, scattering high-fives of snow to road's side, and the kids wave at the driver through the open hatch-window to say their 'Hi!' too. Before we step out for the mandatory snowball fight: galumphing around, sinking to our shins in the chill, lovely stuff—as a willy wagtail meanwhile much more delicately gads about at the edge of a pool of snow-melt.

At hut's rear I discover an eco pit-toilet of roofless design, its seat a furred omega of the purest, soft-fallen snow: like some piece of found-art, the shape of a fleecy angel's wing. (Surreal!) And before wrecking the effect by lifting it, I call the family in to witness this wondrous thing, and take a photograph.

Life brims with such windfalls as these, found casually roadside just two hour's drive south of our suburban Canberra home. Fitting your first set of snow-chains, exchanging a snowplough's high-five, encountering Dali in a toilet seat. Or observing a wagtail's brisk, mystic business: prinking fresh-fallen snow with its perfect, temporary imprint.

Easter Sunday Morning, 'Nil Desperandum'
(Namadgi National Park) (For J & T)

Pre-dawn, the entire child-tribe crawl from their tents
to muster on the frosty lawn. Then, bleary-eyed—
the smallest coached by parents' cues and sly nudges of torchlight—
set to the hunt. Each child pouncing on their finds
with maverick whoops, squeals and Apache-style war-cries
resounding off the valley heights—till, eventually
assailed the bleached-grass of a flanking hill,
the party halts: to gape down at a scattering of clean,
olive-gleaming scat arrayed around their boots.
Oven-fresh, still steaming almost,
and a respectable match in shape-and-size
for the horde of bright-foiled, thumb-sized eggs each child holds
in the beanie clutched to their beating chest.

This scat (despite what one parent mischievously implies)
is *not* the Easter Bilby's—but that of the Eastern Grey kangaroos:
still visible absconding through grass-trees on a distant slope.
Each leaning like a forward-falling prayer
cupped in the valley's misty hands, this Easter-Sunday morn.
As the sun struggles to gain hold of a facing mountain crest
to splash itself across the chill, blue-grey Namadgi hills.

Eventually, in its own sweet, Namadgi deep-space time,
this sun will penetrate the *pisé*-style settlers hut
and damp row of nylon tents, the pit-toilet and woodheap,
and this entire campsite. Reaching inside and touching warm
the core of each of us, parent and child.
Then finally open up this twisted gully
to brand it with daylight, as the day comes right
with the sacred scent of bacon, eggs and coffee.
Transfiguring this whole mountain valley
on this bitter-cold, Namadgi Easter-Sunday morn.

In Nimmitabel (Or: the Monaro gets its elephant)

(Nimmitabel. 1070m asl. Pop.: 240 humans plus 1 elephant)

Walked in on the back of its Mack rig,
it trawls on past the Memorial's honour-roll
gravely as a catafalque, to slide in beside the Bakery
in the town's big, empty main street.
Where the driver climbs down to unhitch the pads and ropes
then hauls the canvas off,
to unsheathe the full, naked majesty of the beast itself:

>Five tonnes of artfully cast concrete,
>painted a sort of peach-pink
>and arrayed in skimpy lingerie
>of gilded garter-belt. Tiara headband,
>necklace of pendant bells.
>Its great head majestically reared, like Landseer's stag.
>Satellite-dish ears aflap. Curled python-trunk upraised
>and trumpeting. One tusk-tip snapped off
>from its container-ride on the high-seas,
>and polysealed in temporary fix.

Stood dancing there, on its four great, padded feet,
braving the High Country's windsheets
as all eyes consider the bare-faced folly, and surreal poetry,
of so unlikely a thing beached itself here,
this crisp, clear winter morning at the millennium's turn.
This red card day when the sun was momently blocked
in the town's high street, as the big rig crept its way sagely in
under weight of its mysterious, humpbacked load.
And the bald plain bucked, quaked and heaved
all the way out to its distant, snow-capped range:
as the Monaro received its elephant.

Four sketches of Monaro towns

1. Diaspora: Adaminaby Blues

(population: 0; 1017 m asl)

The privileged few sandstock buildings in town
were dismantled stone by numbered-stone.
Some of the better-class weatherboards
had their frames sawn through
to be slowly walked out in two halves on truck-back too.

Every building tried what means of escape
(contacts, cunning, bribe) it could.
So as ever only the poorest were left behind,
to rattle in their chains
and creak on their silty, rickety stumps:
dirging from the lake's depths in an unearthly hum
under the Monaro stars and moon.
Calling to be loaded onto their rescuing transport.

Like the Yazidis, frantically throwing their children
into the helicopters' arms,
to be airlifted from their hard, stony hill.

2. Nimmitabel News (or: Don't frighten the horses)

(population: 240; 1070 m asl)

The restored stone-tower of a flour-mill
which never got its sails up
for fear its whirling shadow
might spook horses on the road.

Westward, the Alps' backbone of snow:
like a hijacked ute-load of Switzerland.

And, in the Bakery's playground:
a life-sized, concrete elephant.
Evidently no cause for fright to passing horses.
(Unlike the old windmill.)

3. Off-season Blues

(Anonymous: population: 1727 out of season; 915 m asl)

Out of season the town's a cot-case:
ageing snow bunnies and alcoholic ski-instructors;
little work of any kind.

The local youth bored, and left to stimulate themselves
by what diversion they might seek or find.
Like the fine burst of inspiration
in which they torched the primary school
one long, slow night last week.

4. Lake Eucumbene Gothic

(Old Adaminaby)

The lake reflects on its past life
as vibrant shops and domiciles.

These days yabbies are the birds
which perch in the drowned, blackened trees.
Rainbow trout meander the silty streets,
like yesterday's cats and dogs.

And, safe beyond the caterwaul
of nipping-yapping Victas,
the village's front yards all run amok
with milfoil and marsh flow,
sedge-herb and duckweed.

SOUTH COAST

Salmon trout

(Moruya Heads)

A big bull seal of a man in Adidas shoes and red tracksuit
has shuffled on his buttocks down the stone breakwall
and onto the rocks below, like a spider tip-tripping across its web.
Then, juggling his dual implements, strains awkwardly
to land the bowed, silver weight of a fish:
swung in a great, dripping arc in transfer
from his rod to his long-handled net.

Clambering his way back up, and laying both devices down
like an outsize billiards-cue and cue-rest,
he reaches in and seizes the fish by its jowls.
Unscrews, and removes the orthodontory of hook—
holds the fish prone on a rock, pulls his knife
and pushes its silver tip deep into the animal's neck.

At this, the fish flails hard—once.
Haemorrhaging from gill to tail,
swimming in a sudden film of red.
Then kicks again: as if a new fish
might swim whole and bodily out of it,
and it just might find sanctuary yet …
But adamantly can't. Instead,
flesh slackening, its life distils to its glassy, round upturned eye,
as if photographing this final, resting moment of itself.

> Fish severed forever from Moruya;
> Moruya forever severed from it.

+++

The fisherman relaxes then, seeming satisfied with this.
Pulls and lights a cigarette, and in answer to my ignorant question,
advises it's a Salmon Trout.

'*Arripis trutta*,' as my *Macquarie* later confirms:
'Australian or native salmon', and 'a popular sport fish'.

Which in retrospect explains
the red tracksuit and running shoes, I guess.
The cigarette sucked lustily sidewards,
and the cocky, owzat gleam in the man's keeper's-eye
as he toppled the fish two-handed, like the ball-snicked bails,
into the plastic bucket at his feet.

Postscript: Sense & consequence

When the salmon was pulled from the sea,
had it been waiting there patiently all that while
for my precise arrival on the breakwall
for the chance to offer itself?

Did my walking the length of Bengello
precipitate the fisherman's taking of it?

Or (as I suspect): was the entire bloody business
between salmon, rod, and my arrival on the breakwall
just pure coincidence.
With no remote connection (algorithmic nexus)
between the three discrete parts of this event at all?

Beach house

(Broulee)

[The bungalow]

This house sits slender and light-boned on its beach block,
as architecture in such a privileged spot should.
A simple 1970s construct of corrugated iron and pinewood,
from the sandy drive it appears transparent almost,
as you look straight through the lounge's big picture-window
to the gnarled, old-man banksia in the sandy backyard.
Opening front and back doors creates a cross-breeze,
with the lorikeets heard chortling from both gardens in stereo,
as the house's décor edges in at you in an Asian tease:
a knee-high, stone Buddha-head set in the patio's potted ferns;
batik wall-hangings; and five different styles of triangular cane hat
hung along the hall wall ... As relentlessly, all the while,
the Pacific sends its waves tripping in to shore
just a minute's walk down the dippy, blonde track through the dunes,
a half-dozen doors up the street.

[aka 'Greedy' & 'Gutser']

The Pacific trips in to shore, just a half-dozen doors up the street.
And this sandy garden of bottlebrush, hakea, grevillea and loquat,
attracts a vast number of birds. Rainbow lorikeets, foremost
and dominantly. A technicolour frenzy infesting the place,
voracious and hoarse as they devour flower and fruit.
Specifically one pair we dub 'Greedy' and 'Gutser' for our stay:
with the female (I think) taking the lead, spreadeagling herself
to the kitchen-door's mesh. Evil-eye glimmering in,
as she banshee-shrieks and bullies us over ratty, clinging claws.
Then, when we relent to pour more seed into the tray,
the male comes grappling down through the hakea,
fist-over-beak-over-hand, to join in the feast too.
Here in the garden of this light-filled house sat pat by the breaking shore.
Set slender and light as a gull's bleached bones, on its sandy block.
Just as a house should in such privileged surrounds, but too rarely will do.

Crow

Beating its heavy, Lancaster-like way, out over the dunes
and onto the waves beyond, the eagle has clutch of a small,
dark bundle in its grappling claws
as it's tail-chased (dive-bombed) by a hapless crow.
Harassed further out over the sea—till the crow,
as if suddenly grown less certain of itself
over the new, slippery terrain below,
drops off and wings back, to lodge itself
in a big banksia fringing the shore.

At this, the eagle slowly circles back too:
lumbering toward the bare, upper branches of a tall gum.
And passing straight over us en route, so we glimpse what appears
to be a baby crow, cupped in its big, raptor hands.
Like something dangerously snagged in a bomb-bay's doors.

At Mogo Zoo (The rhino, the meerkats)

The rhino is stood in its paddock enclosure
like a Pajero missed the parking lot.
The sole, fine aspect of the brute
being the big, fleshy section (belly, stifle, fore-shank?)
which curls like leathery art-nouveau
in front of its two, pool-table hindlegs.
And imparting a curiously lissome pose
of ballerina elegance.
True too, when viewed from the rear—
as it saunters the inside perimeter of concrete-and-
steel posts, on slowly lifting pads—
the creature's gait is surprisingly delicate too.
Tripping and meticulous: as if walking a tightrope;
or being chary of damaging the nails of its fresh-painted, outsize toes.

Comparatively, the meerkat is a prospect
of profoundly different type-and-scale of course.
Showing off its communal arrangements and games
in its glass-sided enclosure beside the café.
Sentinel animal hauled erect on its fibreglass-mound:
bandit face, and limp-dick paws; pert, ratty ears
and bristling snout. Hillbilly-head snapping right-left-right,
and diminutive shoulders hunched, like a pearl-diver's kicking up for air.
Glittering-black, crack-addict eyes feverishly working its compound
of PVC tunnelways and wider surrounds.
As if on guard that the rhino hasn't escaped,
to run amok through the landscaped paths.
Come gunning to impale our bespoke date scones,
soy muguccinos and us.

       (*Pace* please, rhinoceros.
              Molto grazie for your concern, meerkat.)

Gulls' hornpipe

(Bermagui)

At a riverside bench,
a big yellow-fin tuna
is being assiduously sliced and honed
from the bone
into red steaks,
each the size, shape and weight
of an ox tongue.
Then laid, one-by-one, on ice
in a Tupperware box.

It's a vernacular sacrament. A romance of its kind.
And you can see how the fisherman's quietly proud
as he works. Cuts, trims,
and then finally scrapes up
and tosses the lights to the gulls …

Who are likewise thrilled to involve themselves,
and play their happy part in this work.
Fierce eyes, big, red, plashing feet,
as they're induced to caper and sing.
And dance the Bermagui Hornpipe.

Sea salmon's ovation

A sea eagle smacks hard at the water
to claw a salmon up—
then mounts on gawping, fletched elbows,
grappling this slippery prize.

All Heaven set on its gleaming back,
as green fields running down
to the cliff's jagged edge,
resound like timpani-rolls all around.

And the ignorant fish flashes silverly,
quakes and flails in its wild applause:

enthralled by the sheer novelty and giddy thrill
of its sudden, unexpected rise

The fleet

Eden isn't mythical, but hard-bruised, raw,
and utterly of this world—you think to yourself,
looking down onto the rucks of fishing boats moored
by the concrete fuel-terminal at Snug Bay wharf.

Big-hitters, these small craft. Curt, brusque, business-like
and practical. Functional of cut and design,
by bald daylight their alien sight can strangely chasten you.
Luminous, and strangely beautiful,
in their blistered war-paint and array of sea-parts—
from salt-scoured, fluoro-coloured nets,
floats and gaffing hooks, to whiplash radio masts.
Which all sing of the bitter elements,
and the place where they go to work each night
in calm and storm alike.

Merimbula, 20 kilometres north, is a rut of clubs,
motels, boutique shops and restaurants—
but Eden, aching and sore from recent hard times,
remains remorselessly real. Lean, nuggetty.
Holding on steadfast. Hardcore.
Its sea-scored flesh pared close to the bone
and stinging like a wound from a slipped fishing knife—
as it trails its simple work song.
Kicking arse from the wet, hose-snaked, concrete floor
of the Fishing Co-op's cold store—
all the crooked way up along Imlay Street.

The crèche

(Whales, Twofold Bay)

The cow huddles hard by her calf
as it toys and tests itself—
then lifts its kitchen-table-sized flukes
to expose its pale-white, heart-shaped under-tail
as it dives.

An adult group lolls in a ring nearby
like outsized Shire horses
in a dissolved corral.
Rolling with stumpy fins up
in the sea's slow, slovenly striptease.
Disclosing only such small, separate parts
as they will.

Snorting, snuffling blowhards,
sunk deep in the vivid flesh-mess of themselves
in the bay's choppy grey slop-&-slurry.

Feeling safe as houses in this harbour these days,
as the chip-mill's big, humpbacked glittering heap
bleeds bright-red through slanting rain
on the headland behind.

Community

(Eden Whale Festival Parade, October)

After the mandatory Scottish pipe band,
and the Primary School float of a killer whale
(masked kids sat straight-and-proud
clutching awry cardboard cut-outs
on benches in the ute's back) ...
And the High-School's dawdling, more surly formulation of same ...
And the Guides-&-Scouts float (with no actual, coherent whale motif
or trope at all, that I discern) ...
And the Breast-Cancer Women's dragon boat
towed by the plasterer's SUV—
with the crew turned out as nuns,
and red-wigged Mother Superior raising a lusty lash to them
at craft's rear.

After these, and more multifarious, whaley carryings-on,
comes a procession of a half-dozen forestry trucks:
hazard lights blinking like flurries of tumbling, tangerine snow
to form up one long, urgent, crippled thing.
Tripping stately and slow as a catafalque
along the crowd-choked street.

       Dad at the lead cabin's wheel,
       young mum like a beaming prom-queen alongside,
       with two kiddies perched on her lap
       and waving royally down on us.

       All squeezed tight together up there on the prime mover's seat,
       with nowhere to go.
       Caught between the history of The Timber & The Whale.
       The present-failing industry,
       and long-since disavowed and failed old.

Afterword

These poems, focussing on the city of Canberra and adjacent mountain regions (the Monaro/High Country), and the southern coast of New South Wales, derive from living in the capital for two decades since arriving with my wife and young children in 1997. Some were published in journals or newspapers as much as 12 years ago, while a few were written to purpose in the last few months of putting this collection together ('Sacrificials 1 and 2', for instance, to pick up on the ideas of ritual sacrifice in the poem 'Blótmonath'). In addition to the poems gathered here, a number of other city-and-region poems were published in two earlier collections, *The Impatient World* and *A Constellation of Abnormalities*.

As I gathered and revised the poems for this collection I became increasingly attuned to the number of connections and cross-currents across them—not just the obvious recurring images (kangaroos, cockatoos, Lake Burley Griffin, 'The [Canberra] Plan' and the like), but also more subconscious and serendipitous recurrences. I decided to run with these: letting the poems tangentially 'speak to' or take strain against each other, giving the collection a thematic cohesiveness and continuity nudging just a little in the direction of a 'livre composé' of sorts.

In terms of style and technique, the moods and voices range from 'cooler'-toned observer, through more affectionate (defensive, even sentimental), and on through to the wry, mischievous, gothic/baroque, caustic epigrammatic and pure 'wild and woolly' ('Ode to Skywhale'?). This fits with the general idea of 'chancing your arm' in poetry: of mixing the registers from high to low, to hopefully provide some entertainment along the way. It ties into the concept of poetry as 'game'—whether deadly serious, middle-range, or more pure diddling fun. Technically I am attracted to rhythm—sometimes strong, vigorous and swinging, driving the narrative and attempting to bind sometimes disparate parts together. Often the rhythm is strongly set in a certain speaker's 'voice', as a 'dramatic monologue'. I'm also drawn to doses of internal and half-rhyme, and occasional risky wordplay, as well as the challenge of arresting imagery.

Attempted forms range from more formal (sonnets, double sonnets and 'near'-sonnets), through elegies and odes, to fractured fables/myths and impertinent 'quips'. There is a valuing of the visceral, the visual, and the vernacular—of concrete imagery, and general 'accessibility', as opposed to the more abstract ('bloodless') obscure or ideological. This again connects to an intention of engaging the reader and drawing them in to the poem, as opposed to blocking them or overly trying their patience. I reckon that wit and humour by no means exclude possibilities of complexity of emotion and feeling. (Personally, I'm sometimes daunted by what seems the unnecessary earnestness of some collections, which deploy not a single instance of humour (either light or dark), or even just the occasional wry observation—let alone the chance of a chuckle, snort, or laugh-aloud hoot.) For me, a fundamental attraction of poetry remains the delight and surprise of taking a line for a walk. Poetry is a fit arena for encountering various types and shades of 'play', every bit as much as any of the other art forms

Notes

'The Plan' ('National Capital Plan'), referred to across this collection: a strategic outline for Canberra and the Territory recognising its unique purpose, setting, character and symbolism as the centre of National Capital functions and as a symbol of Australian national life and values. These 'values' include respect for the key elements of Walter Burley and Marion Mahony Griffins' formally adopted plan. The Plan promotes development which 'respects environmental values and reflects national concerns with the sustainability of Australia's urban areas'. (Which some might think would scotch current proposals for domestic drone delivery services in Canberra's bushy suburbs.) [Source: website of the National Capital Authority, at www.nca.gov.au/planning-heritage/national-capital-plan]

p. 7, 'Blótmonath' (blōtmōnaþ). Anglo-Saxon, from blót = a ritual sacrifice ('blood'); monath = month. (November, ie late autumn, in northern hemisphere.)

p. 31. 'Ode to Skywhale'. *Skywhale* was a balloon artwork approx 23 metres tall by 34 metres nose-to-tail, made of 3500 metres of fabric, and weighing 500 kilograms with fuel, pilot and two passengers on board. Commissioned from former-Canberran sculptor/installation artist Patricia Piccinini, it was unveiled in May 2013 for the Canberra Centenary celebrations. With design, construction and testing costs amounting to $170,000 (plus costs for educational materials and piloting), the piece proved provocative, with some arguing that a more 'beautiful', festive and 'accessible' kind of dirigible might have been preferable. The balloon had its own Twitter account, sending out tweets over the period of its 'performance'.

p. 41, 'Gridlock arrives in the capital'. Prime Minister at the time, John Howard, controversially elected to reside at Kirribilli House on Sydney Harbour rather than in Canberra's official prime ministerial residence, 'The Lodge'.

p. 45, 'Wetsuit: the corrections': reference to 'Grasshopper': affectionate term for novitiate monk deriving from 1970s American Western television series, *Kung Fu*.

p. 49, 'Weereewa (aka "George")'. 'Weereewa' or 'Weereewaa', trans: 'Bad Water'.

p. 50, 'Double-take: Chaplin encounters "King" Yates on Lake George'. In 1930, 'King' Yates attained a speed of 74 mph (119 kph) on a dry Lake George aboard a Harley-Davidson motorcycle. (*Lake George: The biography*, Graeme Barrow, 2012.) Contrary to the poem's implication, Charlie Chaplin, who portrayed a 'famished miner' famously eating a (licorice) boot in a scene in *The Gold Rush* (1925), never actually visited Lake George, or indeed Australia, at all.

p. 57, 'Daytrip to the snowfield'. Original Sawyers Hill Hut, built early 1900s. Subsequently destroyed in 2003 Canberra bushfires and replaced.

p. 58, 'Easter Sunday morning, "Nil Desperandum"'. 'Nil Desperandum': 'Do not (or never) despair': a small farm dwelling built in the pisé or 'rammed earth' style in the 1890s by George Green & George Hatcliff for farmer, eccentric and writer-of-verse Henry Ffrench Gillmann. Property absorbed into the Tidbinbilla Nature Reserve (ACT National Parks) 1991; and subsequently receiving extensive repair following the Canberra Bushfires of January 2003.

pp. 60-61, 'Four sketches of Monaro towns': 'Diaspora: Adaminaby Blues'. Original township flooded by damming of Eucumbene River and construction of Lake Eucumbene as part of the Snowy Mountains Scheme. (Part of original township relocated, 1957.) In drought conditions, original township and relics of the old valley re-emerge from the waters of the lake. 'Nimmitabel news': Geldmacher Mill, hand built by its owner, John Geldmacher, a naturalised German settler in the late 1860s, and completed ready for use in 1872. 'Off-season Blues': Original township transferred to present location in the 1960s prior to damming of Snowy River and construction of Jindabyne Dam.

Acknowledgements

I am indebted to artsACT for a Project Funding Grant which facilitated the writing or revising of many of these and other Canberra-region poems back in 2011. I also wish to thank: Jon Stanhope, who in his long term as Chief Minister of the ACT promoted the city's arts generally; the *Canberra Times* for its long-term publishing of poetry in its weekend Panorama section; Geoff Page for his ceaseless championing of poetry in Canberra in so many ways. And Shane Strange, publisher at Recent Work Press, for editorial advice on the poems, and for valiantly getting up another small press, lifeblood to poetry's survival in this country.

Some of these poems won or were shortlisted for prizes (some resultantly appearing on the artsACT and Two Fires Festival websites):

'Bushfire Season: The comedians': Winner, Braidwood Two Fires Festival Poetry Competition 2007

'Cockatoo Evening' and 'Captain Cook Water Jet' (shortlisted, Poetry in ACTion 2007)

'Coxwain's story': commissioned, Poetry in ACTion 2011, resultantly appearing as a poster on ACT buses in 2011

'Salmon trout, Moruya Heads', Commended, David Campbell Award 2010

'Kosciuszko Report': longlisted, David Campbell Prize

Earlier versions of some of these poems have appeared in journals, newspapers and online:

'Bushfire Season: The comedians', Braidwood Two Fires Festival website

'Salmon trout, Moruya Heads', ACT Past Poetry Prize Award list, Libraries ACT website

'Bermagui Hornpipe', *Canberra Times*

'Rusty', *Canberra Times*

'Captain Cook Water Jet' (Pedal-boat), *Canberra Times*

'The Crèche', *Canberra Times*

'Lake George (aka Weereewaa)', *Meanjin* (special 'Canberra Centenary' issue, 2013)

'Getting the Drift', *Capital Letters* anthology (Boris Books; produced for the annual ANU Poets Lunch, 2008)

Paul Cliff is a Canberra-based poet, playwright and editor. He has worked as Senior Editor in the publications sections of the National Library of Australia and the National Gallery of Australia. This is his fifth book of poetry (in addition to three chapbooks). His last collection, *A Constellation of Abnormalities,* won the ACT Publishing Award for Poetry in 2018. Among other awards and prizes, he has won the David Campbell Poetry Award, while his experimental play, *Deadline: A Manual for Hostage-Taking*, won the Canberra Playwright's Award 2000 and was produced by Canberra Repertory at Canberra's Theatre 3.

2019 Editions
Palace of Memory: An elegy **Paul Hetherington**
Acting Like a Girl **Sandra Renew**
A Coat of Ashes **Jackson**
Summer Haiku **Owen Bullock**
A Common Garment **Anita Patel**
Giant Steps: Reflections on Apollo 11 and beyond **Various**
Some Sketchy Notes on Matter **Angela Gardner**
Canberra Light **Paul Cliff**
A Wardrobe of Selves **Peter Bakowski**
Breathing in Stormy Seasons **Stephanie Green**
Strange Creatures **Alyson Miller**

2018 Editions
The Uncommon Feast **Eileen Chong**
Inlandia **KA Nelson**
Peripheral Vision **Martin Dolan**
The Love of the Sun **Matt Hetherington**
Moving Targets **Jen Webb**
Things I Have Thought to Tell You Since I Saw You Last **Penelope Layland**
The Many Uses of Mint **Ravi Shankar**
Abstractions **Various**
ACE: Arresting, Contemporary stories by Emerging Writers **Various**

all titles available from

www.recentworkpress.com

www.ingramcontent.com/pod-product-compliance
Lightning Source LLC
Chambersburg PA
CBHW032048290426
44110CB00012B/1000